BUTLER AREA PUBLIC LIBRARY
BUTLER, PA.

GIVEN BY

Bucks for Books

Butler Area Public Library
218 North McKean Street
Butler PA 16001

What Is a Family?

THE CHANGING FACE OF MODERN FAMILIES

Adoptive Parents
Blended Families
Celebrity Families
Families Living with Mental
& Physical Challenges
First-Generation Immigrant Families
Foster Families
Gay and Lesbian Parents
Grandparents Raising Kids
Growing Up in Religious Communities
Kids Growing Up Without a Home
Multiracial Families
Single Parents
Teen Parents
What Is a Family?

What Is a Family?

Sheila Stewart

Butler Area Public Library
218 North McKean Street
Butler PA 16001

Mason Crest Publishers, Inc.

Copyright © 2010 by Mason Crest Publishers. All rights reserved. No part of this publication may be reproduced or transmitted in any form or by any means, electronic or mechanical, including photocopying, recording, taping, or any information storage and retrieval system, without permission from the publisher.

MASON CREST PUBLISHERS INC.
370 Reed Road
Broomall, Pennsylvania 19008
(866)MCP-BOOK (toll free)
www.masoncrest.com

First Printing

9 8 7 6 5 4 3 2 1

ISBN 978-1-4222-1528-9
ISBN 978-1-4222-1490-9 (series)
Library of Congress Cataloging-in-Publication Data
Stewart, Sheila.

Produced by Harding House Publishing Service, Inc. www.hardinghousepages.com
Interior Design by MK Bassett-Harvey.
Cover design by Asya Blue www.asyablue.com.
Printed in The United States of America.

Although the families whose stories are told in this book are made up of real people, in some cases their names have been changed to protect their privacy.

Photo Credits

Centers for Disease Control and Prevention 21; Creative Commons Attribution ShareAlike: nerdcoregirl 10; Dreamstime: Noel Powell 9, Galina Barskaya 30, Glenda Powers 33; iStockphoto: d_rich 18

Contents

Introduction   6
1. What's the Difference Between a Traditional and a Nontraditional Family?   8
2. Nontraditional Families Throughout History   17
3. What Makes a Good Family?   29
4. The Expanding Definition of Family   42
Find Out More   60
Bibliography   62
Index   63
About the Author and the Consultant   64

WHAT IS A FAMILY?

Introduction

The Gallup Poll has become synonymous with accurate statistics on what people really think, how they live, and what they do. Founded in 1935 by statistician Dr. George Gallup, the Gallup Organization continues to provide the world with unbiased research on who we really are.

From recent Gallup Polls, we can learn a great deal about the modern family. For example, a June 2007 Gallup Poll reported that Americans, on average, believe the ideal number of children for a family to have these days is 2.5. This includes 56 percent of Americans who think it is best to have a small family of one, two, or no children, and 34 percent who think it is ideal to have a larger family of three or more children; nine percent have no opinion. Another recent Gallup Poll found that when Americans were asked, "Do you think homosexual couples should or should not have the legal right to adopt a child," 49 percent of Americans said they should, and 48 percent said they shouldn't; 43 percent supported the legalization of gay marriage, while 57 percent did not. Yet another poll found that 34 per-

Introduction

cent of Americans feel a conflict between the demands of their professional life and their family life; 39 percent still believe that one parent should ideally stay home with the children while the other works.

Keep in mind that Gallup Polls do not tell us what is right or wrong. They don't report on what people should think—only on what they do think. And what is clear from Gallup Polls is that while the shape of families is changing in our modern world, the concept of family is still vital to our sense of who we are and how we interact with others. An indication of this is the 2008 Gallup poll that found that three out of four Americans reported that family values are important, while one in three said they are "extremely" important.

And how do Americans define "family values"? According to the same poll, here's what Americans say is their definition of a family: a strong unit where faith and morals, education and integrity play important roles within the structure of a committed relationship.

The books in the series demonstrate that strong family units come in all shapes and sizes. Those differences, however, do not change the faith, integrity, and commitment of the families who tell their stories within these books.

WHAT IS A FAMILY?

1 What's the Difference Between a Traditional and a Nontraditional Family?

Terms to Understand

biological: related by blood, genetically.
anthropologists: people who study human cultures and behaviors.
perception: the way things are seen.
scholars: people who study and who have a lot of knowledge on a topic.
sociological: having to do with social issues, especially ones involving culture.
composition: how things are put together and what they are made up of.

Maybe you've heard politicians talking about the "decline of the traditional family." Maybe someone you know talks a lot about how the family isn't what it used to be and how "traditional family values" don't seem to matter anymore. But what do these people mean? What is a traditional family, anyway?

For most people, a traditional family is one with a married man and woman and their children, all living in the same house. A lot of families fit this definition, but many, many families do not. Plus, for some people, the idea of the traditional family means more than this. It might

1 • What's the Difference Between a Traditional and a Nontraditional Family?

What could be more typical that this drawing of the typical nuclear family depicting a mother, a father, two kids and a dog?

mean as well that the father goes to work and the mother stays at home and looks after the home and the children. It might mean the family has a certain number of children. It usually leaves out parents that have divorced and remarried others. Same-sex parents and their children are definitely left out of the traditional family definition.

A nontraditional family, therefore, is one that doesn't meet the definition of two married parents and their *biological* children. The further a family gets from this definition, the more likely it is to be called nontraditional.

WHAT IS A FAMILY?

Do you see a family here? This may not be the traditional American family, but these men have chosen to adopt, raise and love this child—in other words, they have chosen to be a family.

You've probably heard of the nuclear family. This refers to parents and children living together in the same house. Even when people accept other family forms, in North America the nuclear family is often thought of as the ideal. A nuclear family is a unit, one that, supposedly, can meet all the needs of its members, without much help from outside people.

The term "nuclear family" hasn't been around all that long. **Anthropologists** in the first part of the twentieth century were the first ones to use it. They argued that the nuclear family was the most important unit of society.

1 • What's the Difference Between a Traditional and a Nontraditional Family?

The next step out from the nuclear family is the extended family. This includes aunt and uncles, grandparents and cousins. In many cultures, the extended family is just as important as the nuclear family. In some countries, several generations live together in the same house, the younger members helping the oldest ones, while the older ones in turn help teach the younger ones, passing along their wisdom. In Western culture, many people would consider families that live together like this to be nontraditional.

Studies have been done showing that children raised in nontraditional, non-nuclear families do not do as well overall. The **perception** is that when children grow up in nontraditional families, they are lacking something in their lives.

The trouble with these studies is that they don't show the whole picture. Families are complicated things, and the fact that a family is traditional or nontraditional usually has less effect on how well children turn out than other factors in their lives, such as how their parents or guardians interact with each other and with them. Studies mean *something*, of course, but it's usually a good idea to think about *why* they found the results they did. What else might be going on that would also help explain the results?

Some **scholars** believe that calling nontraditional family forms "families" takes away the meaning of the word. Whether you agree with this or not depends on what you

> "Traditional Family Values" is a phrase politicians like to use. People with different political views mean different things by the phrase, but they always mean standards and morals they fear will disappear if their opponents take power.

WHAT IS A FAMILY?

think a family is, how you would define it. If, by family, you mean only a married man and woman and their children, all living in the same house, you probably would agree. If, on the other hand, you would define family as a group of people who are connected to each other biologically, legally, or emotionally—related to each other by birth, adoption, marriage, or love—you might think expanding the definition of family is only right.

What Do You Think?

Explain your definition of what makes a family. Based on what you have read in this chapter, explain in what ways the words "values" and "family" have become connected in people's minds. How would you define "family values"?

HEADLINES

(from "Keeping a Traditional Family Afloat in a Non-Traditional World," by LA Byline, August 30, 2005. Associated Content. http://www.associatedcontent.com/article/8659/keeping_a_traditional_family_afloat.html?singlepage=true&cat=7)

Reared as part of the baby boom generation, my husband and I both came from traditional two-parent families, families that included married parents and

1 • What's the Difference Between a Traditional and a Nontraditional Family?

multiple siblings. In those now distant days, traditional families were the norm. Among my own classmates, it was rare to find one with divorced parents or a step-parent or with another relative as head of the house. Today, however, the trend has turned and my children are the exception among their classmates because they come from a traditional family.

In completing the back-to-school paper work for my elementary age children, I noted that the forms were geared toward the non-traditional family. Blanks were indicated to inform the school which parent was the custodial parent, options to check a box marked "step" before a parent's name, and spaces to indicate with whom does the student reside. There were options for a non-parent guardian to complete and for other relatives who might be raising the child. I applaud the form for being broad because families are made in many forms but there was no space to easily indicate that my children come from a home in which their birth parents are married to one another. I suppose that school personnel will read between the lines to determine this but the form was confusing for our simple situation.

My children were also an exception because they had not attended pre-school until the summer before kindergarten and that only so that they could adjust to a classroom experience. They have not ever had

WHAT IS A FAMILY?

a babysitter who was not a close relative nor been to day care. Because I am able to work at home as a freelance writer, there has been no need but the fact that they remained at home from birth separates them from most of their peers.

Classmates ask about their step-parents or step-siblings only to display shock when there are none. My children carry their father's surname as do I - with my maiden name added on for career reasons. Some of the children that play with my children have siblings with different last names as well as a parent. A surprising number of their fellow students live with a grandparent, aunt or uncle, or other relative. Many seldom see one parent or the other; others are part of a vicious custody battle or a war for affection. And, although many blended families work well, others don't. It's a sad fact in our culture today. . . .

With such *sociological* change since our own childhoods, my husband and I have developed a few tips for those others rearing a traditional family.

Stick to the plan. When you fill out school forms, if there's nothing to indicate that the child's two parents are married to one another, ink it in. Don't be shy about mentioning your family when you're having a haircut, walking the dog, or meeting other adults socially.

1 • What's the Difference Between a Traditional and a Nontraditional Family?

Stay together. There are some old adages that say "the family that stays together prays together". The same goes for eats together, plays together, and rides together.

Teach your children that families are fine no matter who makes up the family circle. Mom, Dad, and the kids are as acceptable as dad and son, a same sex couple raising kids, a single mother and children, a grandparent raising a beloved grandchild, an aunt who adopted a child, and all other situations. Each creates a family. Just because yours is considered traditional doesn't mean that other options aren't okay.

Talk. Open communication is one of the things that keeps our family together and strong.

Laugh. Never forget how to laugh, how to have fun, and how to play.

Keep it light when strangers inquire about the family *composition* and assume that one parent is a stepparent. Explain that some families are still traditional and that it's okay.

Most of all, be a family. I have no idea how the world may be when my children become parents and I am a grandparent but I know that the family—traditional or not—will survive. It's human nature.

WHAT IS A FAMILY?

What Do You Think?

Put in your own words what the author of this article believes about family. Do you agree with this author that families, in whatever shape or form, will always be around—or do you feel that families are at risk in today's world? Explain your answer.

2 Nontraditional Families Throughout History

When people talk about traditional versus nontraditional families, the idea seems to be that families are just now changing into something they have never been before. After all, "traditional" means "according to tradition," or, in other words, something that has been done the same way for a long, long time. So if that's the case, exactly *when* was this time of traditional families?

One likely answer to that question is the 1950s and early '60s, in North America. After World War II, people wanted **stability** in their lives. They wanted a good life. During the war, many women had worked outside of the home. They had filled positions left empty by men fighting

Terms to Understand

stability: staying the same, not changing very much.
domestic: focused on the home and the household.
controversy: disagreement among the public on a matter of opinion.
ideal: perfect, excellent, the best.
era: a period of time set apart by a set of unique characteristics.
myth: a popular belief that is not true or is unproven.
norm: a general average or standard.
annulled: cancelled, made invalid.
constellations: groupings.
oppressed: burdened, troubled, weighed down.
unweaned: a child who does not regularly eat solid foods and still needs her mother's milk to survive.
exploitation: use, especially for one's own profit.

WHAT IS A FAMILY?

After World War II, more women stayed home while their husbands went out to work. However, the idyllic image of the ideal 1950s housewife and family was not reflected in reality.

overseas and they had built airplanes in factories. After the war, however, the soldiers came home, wanting little more than a house, a well-paying job, a *domestic* wife, and a few well-behaved children. Many women left the workplace and focused on being good wives and mothers. Television shows like *Leave It to Beaver*, *The Donna Reed Show*, and *The Dick Van Dyke Show* reinforced these values.

2 • Nontraditional Families Throughout History

In the world of 1950s America, as shown on a television show, men went to work and women cared for the home and the children. Women usually wore dresses—although Mary Tyler Moore caused some **controversy** when she wore capri pants on *The Dick Van Dyke Show*. The father was wise and kind, but stern when it came to discipline. The main couple on the show were happily married and slept in separate beds. *Leave It to Beaver* did have one episode that dealt with divorce, in which Beaver learned that his friend Chopper was going to have a difficult life because of his parents' divorce and their unstable relationships with other people—but that was as far from nontraditional as these shows were willing to venture.

But was life really like that? Well, maybe. For some people.

Even in the 1950s and 60s, all families did not have two happily married parents, raising their own biological children. The *Leave It to Beaver* episode about Chopper and his divorced parents shows that even in 1960, when the episode aired, divorce was common enough to be talked about on a popular family series.

No family is perfect, either now or in the past. Every family has its own share of troubles and issues with which it deals.. For example, the fathers of many of those *Leave It to Beaver*-era families had fought in World War II as young men. Some were emotionally scarred by their experiences in the war and found it

WHAT IS A FAMILY?

difficult to connect with their families. This is not to say that all, or even most, of these war veterans had trouble as fathers, but it is just an example of some of the issues going on beneath the surface that we don't usually think about.

Stephanie Coontz, in her book *The Way We Never Were*, argues that there was no **ideal** time for the "traditional" family. She writes that as people try to think of when the traditional family was at its best, they pick and choose which parts of the past they want to remember, mixing good parts from one **era** with good parts from another, so that they create a **myth** instead of reality. And, of course, television did not usually give an accurate view of life.

So, what were the "nontraditional" families like through history? Were they accepted in society? Or were their members outsiders?

Up until the last century, the world had a fairly high death rate. Diseases were common, women often died in childbirth, and doctors were not usually able to save people who had been hurt in serious accidents. In some parts of the world, this is still the case today. What this means for the family is that sometimes one or both parents might die, leaving the children to be raised by relatives or others. When one parent died—usually the mother, since death in childbirth was common—the other parent often remarried, introducing a stepparent and sometimes stepsiblings into the family.

> A hundred years or more ago, a "seven-month's child" was a child born prematurely, but sometimes the baby was not premature at all. Instead, everyone agreed to pretend the baby was born early so they wouldn't have to admit the mother had become pregnant before she was married.

2 • Nontraditional Families Throughout History

These blended families were not at all frowned upon. Instead, they were almost expected. In most places and times, the two-parent relationship has usually been the *norm* for families, even when families were nontraditional in other ways.

Maternal mortality rates have declined drastically in the United States over the last century, but in the past it was fairly common for a woman to die in childbirth. In many cases, the father would then remarry, creating a blended family.

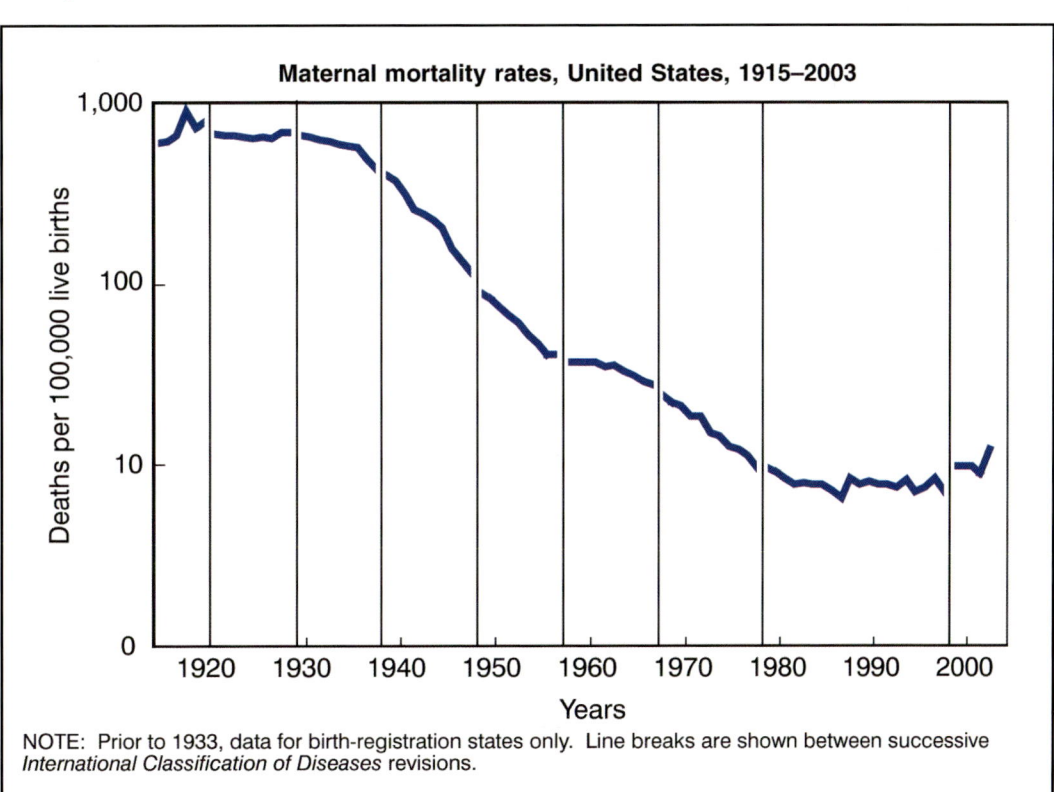

WHAT IS A FAMILY?

Divorce has been rarer than death at creating single-parent or blended families, but it was not unheard of. In Ancient Rome, for example, both men and women usually had the right to divorce. As the Roman Catholic Church gained control over Europe in the Middle Ages, though, the laws against divorce became stricter, until it was forbidden altogether, and a marriage could only be **annulled** by the church if the couple proved they had discovered they were actually closely related to each other.

Like blended families, teen pregnancies were also extremely common throughout history—even in 1950s America!—although sometimes this was because women were often married while still in their teens. Pregnant teenagers were less of

This Renaissance painting of a couple on their wedding day shows that women during the 1500s were sometimes already pregnant when they got married.

2 • Nontraditional Families Throughout History

a scandal in Western Europe over the past thousand years than a pregnancy outside of marriage. Usually, when such a pregnancy happened, either the couple was quickly married or else the woman took a long vacation to visit a distant relative and the baby was quietly adopted by a family member or given to monks or nuns to be raised by the church.

While blended families and teen pregnancies may have been common, some forms of nontraditional families were not. Multiracial families, for example, have usually been frowned on, if not completely forbidden. The children in such multiracial families have often had trouble being accepted by either race. They too often were caught between worlds and didn't seem to belong anywhere.

Same-sex families in history are even rarer than multiracial families. Evidence from the ancient world shows that homosexual relationships were sometimes common and more or less accepted in places like Greece, Rome, and China. The reason these relationships were sometimes controversial even then was that they were not able to produce children—something usually honored throughout history. For this reason, people in a homosexual relationship were likely to also be in a heterosexual relationship. When, at certain periods of history, some people did choose to live only in a same-sex relationship, children were almost never part of the family.

> Traditionally, some Native Americans were two-spirit people. This meant that they had both a male and a female spirit in the same body. Two-spirit people adopted some combination of male and female dress and practices and sometimes served as shamans or in other spiritual or mystical roles. They were found in many different tribes and were accepted members of their society.

23

WHAT IS A FAMILY?

Given to God

Up to the twelfth century it was customary to place boys and girls dedicated to God in monasteries at the age of five or six, and sometimes even earlier. Such a child was called an oblatus, and was offered to God on the altar of the church by his parents, who vowed that, when the time came, their child would become a nun or monk. Until the eighth century, custom dictated that when a boy reached 14 (or a girl, 12), he (or she) could decide whether to become a monk for the rest of his (or her) life. In the eighth century, however, this right was taken away from children, and the parent's commitment became irreversible. Eventually, in the twelfth century, this custom was questioned, and increasing numbers of people came to believe that it was wrong to impose a lifelong obligation on a child. Many also thought that the presence of children in monasteries disrupted normal life there.

Clearly, however, many different kinds of families have been around for centuries. Over the years and around the world, children have been raised in a variety of household settings, while adults have formed emotional connections that were not always based on a marriage commitment. Given that such family **constellations** existed, the next question is this: were these "good"

2 • Nontraditional Families Throughout History

families? Did they help make their members' lives easier and society as a whole stronger?

What Do You Think?

Talk to your grandparents or people you know who were alive during the 1950s and early '60s. Compare what they tell you to the family life you see portrayed on some of the old TV Land shows. How accurate do you think these shows were? Do you think these television shows still influence the way we think about family today? Why or why not?

HEADLINES

(From "Books of The Times; A Mystery of Humanity From the Middle Ages," by Caryn James, *The New York Times*. February 15, 1989. http://www.nytimes.com/1989/02/15/books/books-of-the-times-a-mystery-of-humanity-from-the-middle-ages.html?scp=3&sq=middle%20ages%20children&st=cse)

According to a 13th-century Spanish law, "A father who is *oppressed* with great hunger or such utter poverty that he has no other recourse can sell or pawn his children in order to obtain food." A first-century writer describes certain pillars at a public market in Rome as nursing columns because *unweaned* infants were so often abandoned there. And in the sixth cen-

25

WHAT IS A FAMILY?

tury children were so frequently left at churches that a book of fill-in-the-blank model letters included one stating the finder's rights. "Whereas, I, brother ——, one of the dependents of the parish of St. ——," it reads, "found there a newborn infant, not yet named, and was unable to find relatives of his among any of the populace, it was agreed to and permitted by the priest ——, that I could sell the child to ——."

Such documentary evidence, included in John Boswell's study of the abandonment of children from the Roman Empire through the Middle Ages, is certainly chilling but should not be shocking. For if it is not news that children are neglected even now, how much more likely that they would be given up or sold when slavery was a way of life.

"The Kindness of Strangers" holds no hint of *exploitation* about its disturbing subject. Arguing that abandonment was commonplace in these civilized societies, Mr. Boswell plunges into an area with great potential to illuminate what seems to the modern mind like a mystery of human nature. . . .

His major point is that abandoned children were rarely left to die. Parents were often unable to feed their children or feared that too many heirs would destroy an estate by splitting it into tiny pieces—the most common reasons for abandonment. So they

2 • Nontraditional Families Throughout History

placed infants in conspicuous public spaces, often leaving tokens alongside—signs of social status or an object by which children could be identified should parents change their minds. After Christianity arrived, salt was left as a symbol that the child had been baptized. The finders might pass off these foundlings as their own heirs but in imperial Rome were far more likely to turn them into slaves.

Civil and canon laws are Mr. Boswell's best evidence that abandoning and selling children was commonplace. In one of his favorite chicken-or-egg arguments, he says the practice was widespread because it appears so often in imaginative literature, and later he says that imaginative literature deals with abandonment because it mirrors reality. But the many legal citations provide a convincing clue that unwanted children were a major social concern.

Among such sources, he finds no evidence that it was illegal to abandon children or widely considered immoral, even in Christianity. The aftermath, not the abandonment, was the thorniest issue. Could freeborn children who were found be enslaved? Not legally, but that situation was hard to prevent. Could parents reclaim their children? Often they could but had to repay maintenance costs to the foster parents. There was rarely any stricter punishment for casting out one's children.

> Khnumhotep and Niankhkhnum were Egyptian royal servants, living at about 2400 B.C.E. The two men were buried together in the same tomb, the walls covered with images of them holding hands and kissing. Many believe them to be the earliest recorded same-sex couple.

WHAT IS A FAMILY?

Mr. Boswell charts some interesting changes in the late Middle Ages. During the 11th and 12th centuries, a period of prosperity, abandonment is scarcely mentioned, suggesting that a stronger economy allowed parents to care for their own children. During the economic and social decline of the 13th century, however, unwanted children became a problem again. By the 14th century, foundling hospitals had been established throughout Europe with tragically ironic results. The mortality rate was extremely high in such institutions, most likely because disease spread so rapidly there.

What Do You Think?

Were you surprised to learn that children were abandoned by their parents centuries ago? Think about the fairy tales you read as a child; these stories were based on everyday life during the Middle Ages. Make a list of "nontraditional" families that appear in fairy tales.

3 What Makes a Good Family?

Terms to Understand

sociologists: people who study human society, how it is organized and how it works.
comprehensive: including many things.
denunciation: the act of condemning or criticizing something publically.
predestined: having the result or action determined in advance, so that it cannot be any other way.
stigma: a mark of disgrace on a person's reputation.
self-fulfilling prophecy: a prediction that causes itself to come true, either directly or indirectly, because people act as though they believe it will come true.
ostracism: being excluded and shut out of social circles.
problematic: raising questions or doubts.
disruption: the act of breaking something apart, causing confusion or chaos.
gravity: seriousness.
besetting: constantly surrounding, troubling, attacking.
predispose: to make someone more likely to deal with something; to give someone a tendency toward something.

All families are different. Take any two families, "traditional" or non-traditional and you'll find huge differences between them—and similarities as well. Families have different likes, dislikes, and habits. They have different issues with which they struggle. They react in different ways to the problems they face.

What makes some families more successful than others? Why do some families enjoy talking to each other, have fun together, and stay strong during the difficult times, while other families seem to scream at each other all the time, have more problems with drug and alcohol abuse, or lie to each other regularly. Are those happier, stronger families "good" and those struggling families "bad"?

WHAT IS A FAMILY?

Families who enjoy spending time together, no matter how different they may be in some ways, have been shown to handle stress better than those who don't get along.

Defining a good family can be tricky. People often judge other families by how they compare to their own, and sometimes the issue is not right or wrong, it's what a person is used to. Maybe the family that screams at each other all the time truly loves each other and would

3 • What Makes a Good Family?

go out of their way to help any other member of the family who needed support. Maybe it's just their communication style that needs work. But someone from a family that hardly ever yells at each other might not realize this.

Sociologists talk about the difference between *form* and *function* when describing what a family is. When a person talks about what a family looks like—if it is made up of two married, opposite-sex parents and their children or an interracial same-sex couple with their adopted child—they are talking about the form of the family. Even things like how much a family yells at each other are more of a question of form.

Function, on the other hand, has to do with how a family works, how well it does what it is supposed to do. People disagree on exactly everything a family is supposed to do, but most would say something like, "A family should raise children to become independent members of society," or, "A family should support each other and be there for each other in good and bad times."

CBBC, the children's branch of the British television broadcaster, asked the question, "What do you think makes a happy family?" and invited viewers to e-mail their answers to the website. Of the dozens of children who answered the question, the ideas that were repeated again and again included spending time together, having fun together, being able to talk to each other, and

WHAT IS A FAMILY?

loving each other. Several also wrote that money didn't have anything to do with a family's happiness. All of their responses had to do with the function of a family and not its form.

The University of Missouri's MissouriFamilies website includes an article called "What Makes a Family Strong?" The article lists six strengths that good families often have. These are:

- Positive mental health in parents—when the parents are calmer and happier, the children tend to be as well.

- Everyday routines—children like knowing what to expect from their families and their home life.

- Spending time together—making time for each other helps family bonds become stronger.

- Communication and praise—being able to tell each other the truth, knowing they can trust the reaction, is important in strong families.

- Monitoring, supervision, and involvement—children like to know their parents care enough about them to set boundaries and make sure they are kept.

- Warm and supportive relationships between the parent and child.

3 • What Makes a Good Family?

In another article from the University of Missouri Extension program, the authors, Gail R. Carlson and M. Kathy Dothage, list a number of tips to help strengthen families. They stress that their list is not "a set of rules that must be followed or . . . a checklist by which you grade your own or other families. Rather, they are tools to aid family discussion and interaction and means of learning more about your family."

A survey done in 2003 found that 40 percent of families eat dinner together no more than three times a week, while 10 percent never eat together at all. Children who regularly eat with their families have been shown to have a lower risk of substance abuse and depression than those who do not.

WHAT IS A FAMILY?

- *All families can be strong and healthy:* "What makes a family strong does not depend on who makes up the family but how well they work together to accomplish necessary tasks, such as meeting individual member's needs, teaching children what is expected of them and how to carry out required tasks, maintaining the family unit, and developing a shared set of meanings, values and goals. Nontraditional families, and that includes most of us, must learn new ways of accomplishing these tasks."

- *Healthy families spend "prime time" together:* "By spending pleasant, positive time together, families build up a reserve of good feelings. When trouble comes it has to be shared with the family and resolved. If the problems are not balanced by shared pleasures, in time, people may come to associate family life with unpleasant rather than pleasant things."

- *Strong families build connections with other families and people.*

- *Strong families plan for change:* "Learning to distinguish between those things we can control and those we can't, and using our energy to change the things we can, is critical to improving the quality of family life."

3 • What Makes a Good Family?

- *In healthy families, members are committed:* "Family members think of each other as friends with whom they can talk and have fun. They enjoy each other as individuals and like being together. They recognize that functioning together as a family is not always easy . . . but they work at making family life more enjoyable and satisfying.

- *Healthy families share responsibility:* "Typically, involvement in planning and decision-making brings with it a commitment to the plan or goal and cooperation in carrying it out."

- *Strong families have shared values and beliefs:* "It is important that the family's values and beliefs are talked about and used in daily situations."

- *Strong families handle conflicts and disagreements constructively:* "In a healthy family where individual uniqueness is being encouraged, disagreements can be expected."

- *Healthy families balance home, work, and outside activities.*

- *In strong families, members show appreciation for each other:* "Being accepted by others helps develop a person's self-concept and generates feelings of being important, loved and appreciated."

WHAT IS A FAMILY?

- *In healthy families, there is effective communication:* "For effective communication to take place, the family must provide an emotionally and physically 'safe' environment."

- *Healthy families realize that effective communication involves effective listening:* "Checking out your interpretation [of what was said] with the speaker, 'getting feedback,' before responding or acting is a good way to reduce misinterpretation."

What Do You Think?

When it comes to families, is it form or function that's most important? Do you think some "forms" encourage better "function"? Why or why not?

3 • What Makes a Good Family?

HEADLINES

(From "What Makes a Happy Family?" by Polly Toynbee, *The Independent*, Jan. 17, 1994. http://www.independent.co.uk/opinion/what-makes-a-happy-family-polly-toynbee-explains-what-research-can-and-cannot-tell-us-about-the-children-of-lone-parents-1407474.html)

In all the debate on the fate of the family, everyone seems to agree that what matters most is what becomes of the children of divorce or single parenthood. Do they fare worse, and if so, by how much and why? And what can be done about it?

The most **comprehensive** survey so far of all the research on this area is published today by the Family Policy Studies Centre. It asks more questions than it answers, but it does suggest that a simple **denunciation** of single parenthood is beside the point. While some children do badly, others do not. Their fate is not **predestined**.

There are serious problems with much of the existing research, which in Britain is mainly based on two big studies, one of a group of children born in 1946 and the other of children born in 1958, followed through at intervals, and now also including their children.

For children growing up in those days, divorce and illegitimacy were relatively rare, so the social **stigma** was greater. Teachers then had lower expectations of these children, which in other research has been

WHAT IS A FAMILY?

shown to be a dangerously *self-fulfilling prophesy*. Born myself in 1946, a child of two divorces, I know that it felt relatively *exceptional*. But classrooms everywhere now are so full of children with complicated families that it must feel very different. So some of the damage done to children by divorce and illegitimacy reported here may be the effect of a social *ostracism* that is out of date.

The more this report explores and compares the many (sometimes sharply conflicting) studies, the more gaping chasms open up in our understanding of the fundamental elements of family life. But it does seem without doubt that, broadly, the children of divorce and single parenthood do worse, in virtually every respect. Divorce and separation are worst of all, single parenthood and subsequent step-parenthood next, with the children of never-married mothers who stay single and widows suffering least harm.

These children do worse at reading and maths, and their parents report more anxiety and bad behaviour. They get lower educational qualifications than would have been expected for their social class, and as a result they get worse jobs later in life.

But that's not the end of the story. While no one seriously questions that happy parents who stay together are likely to produce the happiest children,

3 • What Makes a Good Family?

this report stresses that there is so much variation within groups that it is impossible ever to predict a happy or unhappy outcome for a particular child of any background.

The research implies that the worse the parental conflict, the worse the child will do. Upheaval and disharmony matter far more than the shape of family the child is brought up in. But measuring relative rates of happiness and conflict is, to say the least, *problematic*.

Do we reach the limits of sociology here? A recent British Social Attitudes Survey found that six out of 10 people thought it better for the children if an unhappy marriage were ended. If unhappily married couples want to know how to do the best for their children, they need to know whether staying together unhappily produces better children than divorcing. But how do you set about measuring relative rates of unhappiness in couples who decide to stay married? As with pain thresholds, some people tolerate extreme misery in marriage, while others protest vehemently about apparently trivial levels of dissatisfaction.

The research shows that children of divorce have started to do badly long before the actual separation, and do no worse after it. That suggests that it is conflict, rather than the separation, that may do the most harm.

WHAT IS A FAMILY?

When people divorce, the mother and children come under unusual stress. They are nearly always much poorer than before, moving down the social scale. They often move house, and school. Half the children lose touch with their fathers for ever. Many children suffer further *disruption* on remarriage, not just acquiring a stepfather, but again moving house and school. Some mothers go on to have more children. Yet despite it all, some children do very well.

There is so much that needs measuring. How much does it matter how well siblings get on, or how well children get on with their parents, or with step- parents? What are the measures of "good" relationships which protect children from suffering too much harm? . . .

The most important question is, how bad is the damage? No clear answer emerges here either, but there are indications. Reading age varies according to class, gender, birth weight and family size. One major study looked at children aged seven to 11. "Illegitimate" children were on average found to be 10 months behind the average reading age. How bad is that? Not as bad as coming from a family with three or more siblings, when the child will be 11 months below average. Not all that unlike the natural gender difference, where girls at that age are eight months ahead of boys. In maths, the social class difference

3 • What Makes a Good Family?

between children is nine months, while the difference between legitimate and illegitimate children is five months.

This puts the *gravity* of the problem into some kind of perspective. Is divorce and single parenthood the most important problem *besetting* children of this generation? It may *predispose* them to suffer all kinds of disadvantages, especially poverty, but lots of other children are poor and disadvantaged, too.

What Do You Think?

Do you think divorce and single parenthood is the biggest problem today's children face? Why or why not? This article describes research that has been done in England. Do you think the same results would be found in the United States and Canada?

WHAT IS A FAMILY?

4 The Expanding Definition of Family

Terms to Understand

fluid: changing easily.
communes: small groups of people, outside of traditional family groups, living together and sharing their belongings and money.
harassment: repeated bothering, torment, or attacks.
fluctuating: changing constantly; moving back and forth.
cohabitation: living together.
contract: to pull together into a smaller part.
donor: a person who gives something.
artificially inseminated: when a woman has a man's sperm nonsexually injected into her reproductive tract in order to get pregnant.
anonymous: unknown person; having a person's name or identity kept secret.

People feel very strongly about the meanings of words sometimes. Some believe that if the definition of a word shifts, the reality of the original meaning will be harmed. But the meanings of words change all the time. Language is *fluid*. It always has been. (Think about how much English has changed, for example, since the sixteenth century when Shakespeare was writing!)

When the word "family" was first used, it meant the servants of a household. Not for more than another two hundred years—in the 1660s—did it have the meaning of people who were related by blood. The word "kin," however, did mean people who shared a common "blood,"

4 • The Expanding Definition of Family

who were connected by birth (but those people didn't necessarily share a household). Over the years, the two definitions became mingled, and eventually, the word "family" often came to mean blood relations who share a household.

Today, people argue a lot about the meaning of "family." There are two levels to this argument. On one level, some people are concerned with whether a certain family type is good or bad. In other words, they might say that a two-parent family is good, but a single-parent family is not as good or a family with same-sex parents is not as good.

On the other level of argument, people sometimes ask, "When is a family not a family?" That is to say, when have we stretched and expanded the definition of the word so much that it isn't really true anymore?

To make the answer to that question more complicated is the fact that the meaning of family can be different depending on how you use it and the situation you are in. This is true for a lot of words, of course. Take the word "mouse" for example. Do you mean a furry little creature? A tool for moving the cursor around the computer screen? A shy, quiet person?

Terms to Understand

sperm bank: a place where sperm is stored and kept ready to be used in artificial insemination.
forging: creating, forming.
unanticipated: not expected.
defray: to pay some or all of something.
genealogy: family tree; a record of ancestors and relatives.
piqued: became interested, curious, or enthusiastic.
prodigy: a person who has an extraordinary talent or ability at a unusually young age.
nature vs. nurture: the ongoing argument about how much of a person's character and physical traits come from genetics through their parents (nature) and how much come through their environment and other outside influences (nurture).

WHAT IS A FAMILY?

A hundred years ago, families in America tended to be much larger. Today, a family with twelve children would be considered unusual.

The definitions for "mouse" are different enough that you can tell easily enough from the context which meaning is meant—but "family" can be more difficult when it comes to figuring out which definition is meant.

Legal situations are the most difficult when it comes to defining "family." The law has very specific definitions for things, and these definitions can be different depending on the court system. Legal definitions can also depend on how things were defined originally in a law or a contract.

4 • The Expanding Definition of Family

In 1971, the members of two **communes** in Palo Alto, California, sued the city authorities for **harassment**. The zoning laws said that no more than four people who were not related to each other could live in the same house together. The members of the communes argued that they were actually a family—a "voluntary" family—and that they had a constitutional right to be treated equally with any traditional family.

The judge in the case seemed to find the issue very interesting, although he did not, in the end, side with the communes. He reasoned that although the communes may have functioned as a family to some extent, "There is a long-recognized value in the traditional family relationship which does not attach to the 'voluntary family.'" Also, the judge stated, "Communal living groups are voluntary, with **fluctuating** memberships who have no legal obligations of support or **cohabitation**."

In this case, the judge looked at the reason behind the original law—making sure properties were cared for and rents were paid. He realized that the nature of the commune family was that people came and went from it and that, unlike a more traditional family, there would be no legal way to protect the person whose name was on the lease if the other commune members decided to move on. The author of the *Time* article on the case wondered if the commune could have one or two members adopt the others so they would legally be a family and able to stay.

> Fictive kin is a term used to describe people who are not related to each other by birth or by marriage, but who relate to each other as family. This might include godparents or your parents' friends whom you call "aunt" or "uncle" even though they aren't really related to you.

45

WHAT IS A FAMILY?

In 1994, the same situation came up again in Toledo, Ohio, this time concerning university students rather than commune members. Neighbors worried that too many students living in one house could be loud and disruptive, and the city counsel passed the family-rental ordinance, stating that no more than four unrelated people could share a house. The author of a story on the situation in the *Toledo Blade* wrote that "defining a family is like trying to nail the proverbial Jello to the wall."

Certainly, the definition of family moves around a lot, depending on how you use the word. The meaning can **contract** to mean the nuclear family or expand to include unrelated people who share the same values, interests, or goals and who enjoy spending time together. When a group of friends, for example, functions as a family, they often refer to themselves as one.

The distinction, again, comes down to whether we are talking about defining the *form* of a family or its *function*. Those in nontraditional families usually talk about how their family functions. For those in healthy families, whether traditional, nontraditional, or ones that push the boundaries of the word family into an entirely new territory, love is what ties them together. Love is what makes them a family.

46

4 • The Expanding Definition of Family

What Do You Think?

Are there people in your lives you consider family, even though you're not related? Do you think the law should be required to recognize and honor relationships that are outside the boundary lines of a "traditional" family? In your opinion, how should the word "family" be defined legally?

HEADLINES

(from "Sperm Donor Siblings Find Family Ties," by Daniel Schorn. *60 Minutes*. June 24, 2007. http://www.cbsnews.com/stories/2006/03/17/60minutes/main1414965.shtml?tag=contentMain;contentBody)

All over the United States, new kinds of extended biological families are springing up that no one ever anticipated or dreamed possible. These families are made up of something called "*donor* siblings," and if you don't know what they are, neither did we until we began working on this story.

As correspondent Steve Kroft reports, an estimated 30,000 children are born in this country each year to mothers who have been *artificially inseminated* with sperm from an *anonymous* donor. Most of these children grow up never knowing their biological father—but

WHAT IS A FAMILY?

now, with the help of *sperm bank* records and the Internet, some of them are finding half-brothers and half-sisters they never knew they had, who were sired by the same anonymous donor, *forging* family ties they never knew existed.

Wade Anderson is a pioneer of sorts, an unwitting participant in an *unanticipated* drama. He was conceived four years ago with the help of an anonymous sperm donor, a man that neither he nor his mother, Robin, have ever met.

Robin and her partner, Cindy Brisco, had been together for 15 years when they decided they wanted a child; they went to a San Diego sperm bank, looked through a donor catalog, and paid $320 for two vials from a man identified only as donor "48QAH."

Asked what she was looking for in a donor, Robin Anderson says: "What was important to me, was heart. That the donor had heart. And I didn't know how we were gonna find that."

They knew from 48QAH's profile that he was a doctor, one of many who have helped *defray* the cost of medical school by donating sperm. He described himself as 6'4", 190 pound with brown hair and green eyes and an interest in caring for critically ill children.

4 • The Expanding Definition of Family

"And I thought, this is a sensitive man," Cindy says. "I like this. I like the way this feels. This guy's gotta be deep."

As it turned out, 48QAH proved to be a popular choice. At a party last summer, Robin was introduced to a single mother named Maren, who said she had conceived her daughter, Lila, after a visit to the Fertility Center of California.

"And just then, Cindy walked up. And she said, 'Oh, that's where we went. What donor number did you use?' " Robin recalls.

Cindy told her they had used 48QAH.

"And she said, very calmly, 'That's it.' And we're like, 'What?'" Robin says.

In that moment, the three women realized that this was more than a just a coincidence. Their two children were half-brother and half-sister.

"And to think that this baby girl was his half-sibling," says Robin.

Cindy and Robin say they really consider Wade and Lila to be brother and sister.

"They have each other. They don't have the donor, the father; they have each other," Robin explains.

WHAT IS A FAMILY?

The two children live just 10 minutes apart. Their mothers talk frequently on the phone, get together every few weeks, and say they have begun to raise Wade and Lila as siblings.

"We love Maren, the mother. We love baby Lila. I mean, we have a lot in common. We're a great family match," says Robin.

"But you have to admit this is a little unusual," says Kroft. "I'm still trying to get my mind around it. This is not a traditional family in any stretch of the imagination."

"I mean, what is a traditional family today? I mean, I didn't have a father growing up," Cindy says.

It may seem like something out of "Brave New World," but this extended family of five, with its complicated *genealogy* is not as unusual as you might think.

A decade ago, donor insemination was used almost exclusively by married couples with fertility problems, often keeping the children in the dark. Today, roughly half of the people going to sperm banks are lesbian couples and single women.

With no male in the household, it's harder to conceal the truth, so a generation of donor kids, like Ryan Kramer, has stepped out of the shadows and begun

4 • The Expanding Definition of Family

to seek answers to some of life's most basic questions: who am I, and where did I come from?

Asked why this became so important to him, Ryan says: "Having that half of my family and half of really where I came from be a complete unknown was something that I was very curious about. I feel that I'm a whole person, but I'm missing part of where that person came from."

When somebody asks who his father is, Ryan says he tells people he doesn't know. "I was born through anonymous donor insemination. So, I don't know who he is exactly," he explains.

Asked what he puts down on forms he has to fill out for school, Ryan says, laughing, "N/A (Not Apply)."

Ryan lives outside Denver with his mother, Wendy. She conceived him with an anonymous sperm donor because there were fertility issues with her and her husband. That marriage ended in divorce when Ryan was one. Over time, her son's endless curiosity about his biological father and potential half-siblings *piqued* her own.

"You said that there were traits that obviously didn't come from you. What were the traits?" Kroft asked.

"His brain," Wendy replied, laughing.

WHAT IS A FAMILY?

What makes a father? Are children who share a common sperm donor a "family"?

Ryan is a mathematics *prodigy*. At 15, he is a sophomore at the University of Colorado, studying aerospace engineering. Lots of mothers hope to raise a rocket scientist; Wendy Kramer got one.

She says that didn't come from her. "And I used to joke that, ya know, as far as, ya know, the sperm goes, I put in for regular and somebody gave me high-test," Wendy says.

4 • The Expanding Definition of Family

Hoping to find Ryan's biological father, Wendy contacted her sperm bank. The California Cryobank is one of the largest in the country, and has supplied the sperm to create as many as 200,000 babies. But like other banks, it is built on the bedrock of anonymity, insulating donors from paternal obligation—legal, financial, or otherwise. So Wendy Kramer went to the Internet and began building an online database called the Donor Sibling Registry.

It's a worldwide registry for donor conceived people. Wendy says the response has been huge.

"Adult donor conceived people, parents of the donor conceived and, now more than ever, even the donors themselves are coming to the site saying, 'I had no idea that I had the right to be curious,' " she explains.

The Web site now has more than 7,000 members. They send in their contact information, along with the name of the sperm bank that was used, and the donor number. The Web site collates the information, allowing donors, their offspring, and half-siblings to contact with each other.

On the site, one can spot quite a few matches, highlighted in yellow.

And some of these new family trees can be quite large. It's not unusual for an anonymous sperm do-

WHAT IS A FAMILY?

nor to make multiple deposits in a sperm bank. Some of them, whether they know it or not, have fathered more than a dozen children.

Asked who the record holder is on her Web site, Wendy says one donor has fathered 20 children.

So far, more than 1,600 people have found biological family members through Kramer's Web site they didn't know they had.

"And there've been many stories of people meeting," Wendy says. "First e-mailing on the Internet and then, you know, flying all over the country to meet each other and it's like—it's redefining family. It's making family where there was none."

They are new families like Justin Senk, Erin and Rebecca Baldwin, and McKenzie and Tyler Gibson. Just looking at them you wouldn't know there is anything remarkable about them, aside from a certain family resemblance, until you hear their story.

They're the sons and daughters of three different mothers, and each of them was conceived with the sperm of the same anonymous donor, No. 66 at the Rose Medical Center. The kids met after finding each other online through the Donor Sibling Registry and, incredibly, they all live in the Denver area.

4 • The Expanding Definition of Family

Tyler thinks there is definitely a bond between the five children, beyond the fact they know they are half-siblings.

"Even the first time that we've met each other, it was just kind of like, you know that there's something more to than just knowing who they are," he explains. "There was something else there."

As soon as they met, they noticed striking similarities, more than just the same fair skin and blonde hair

"When I saw McKenzie, my jaw dropped because I was like, 'That looks exactly like I did when I was 11,'" Rebecca remembers.

They share half their DNA, and provide a fascinating study of *nature vs. nurture*. They can see aspects of their personalities reflected in each other—but that only makes them more curious about where it all came from.

"It's always been really interesting to me to know where my personality came from. And, yeah, I see it a lot more in these guys," says Rebecca. "And it's great to have half-siblings, to see that, 'Oh, that's where my personality came from, that.' But it'd be even more interesting to see it straight from the source."

They'd like to see a picture of donor 66, and know why he decided to donate the sperm that helped cre-

55

WHAT IS A FAMILY?

ate them. But unless he decides to step forward, that is not likely to happen. Only a small percentage of donors have shed their anonymity, which is why Robin Anderson and Cindy Brisco were shocked when they went online and saw that their donor had posted a note saying that he was willing to be contacted.

"That night, I clicked on his e-mail. And I said, 'Are you 48QAH? And if you are, I have an incredible child to tell you about,'" Robin recalls.

Behind the mysterious 48QAH was now a face, and a name: Matthew Niedner, a 34-year-old pediatrician living in Ann Arbor, Mich. "QAH," it turns out, stood for "quite a hunk" at the clinic where he had donated sperm for seven years.

Niedner says he got paid about $50 a specimen and estimates he donated between 150 and 200 specimens. Conceivably, he could have more than a hundred children.

Matthew Niedner doesn't know how many children he's fathered, although he thinks it's no more than a couple of dozen.

"If I have information or can answer questions that nobody else can that can help those kids, then I feel very good about participating in trying to bridge that informational gap," Niedner explains.

4 • The Expanding Definition of Family

"I have seen pictures. They e-mailed me some pictures," Niedner says.

Asked if they're good looking kids, Niedner says, laughing, "Well, there's a loaded question."

Niedner began donating sperm when he was single, and continued to do so after he got married. He and his wife, Nicole, are now expecting a child of their own.

What was his wife's reaction when he told her that he had gotten these e-mails?

"Well, I shared them with her and she was ecstatic," Niedner recalls.

Asked if it was delicate in any way, he says: "Yeah. I mean, you know, I tried to be very thoughtful and cautious about the whole thing. But she's been nothing but wonderful and loving and supportive."

Kroft asks: "When you decided to become a sperm donor, did you actually sit down and think that there were going to be babies created out of this and that someday they might try and contact you? Or you might try and contact them?"

"I guess I entertained the possibility of that. You know, I look at it a little differently," Niedner says. "This may sound a little detached, but I don't really look at these children as my children or, you know,

WHAT IS A FAMILY?

that I'm their father. I was somebody who provided a tool or a necessary ingredient for a family to have a child that was wanted."

Niedner says he is not interested in fulfilling any sort of parental role.

"Do you think the children will think that way?" Kroft asks.

"Well, I don't think there's a blanket answer to that. I think different children will feel differently," he says.

His donor children, Wade and Lila, are each growing up without a father, which might make it harder for him to keep his distance.

For now, he's proceeding cautiously, and since the mothers of his donor children have never met Niedner or heard his voice, *60 Minutes* decided to surprise Cindy and Robin with a little video preview.

What did they think?

"He's animated, like my Wade," Cindy says, laughing. "He's cute."

"Kind, you can see the kindness," Robin says. "And look at the eyebrows."

"There is my boy's eyebrows," Cindy adds.

4 • The Expanding Definition of Family

Just this week, they met another donor sibling, Alexandra, a half-sister to Wade and Lila. Their 21st century donor family, made possible by 48QAH, is still growing.

Since Kroft's story first aired in 2006, Cindy and Robin have seen their family grow even larger. Besides those two sisters, they have discovered their son Wade has three half-brothers. Now there are six known children from donor "48QAH." And last summer, Matthew Niedner and his wife had a child of their own—a healthy baby girl.

What Do You Think?

When people talk about "nontraditional families," they're usually referring to people who consider themselves to be family despite the fact that they're not related biologically—but this article describes a different kind of nontraditional families: ones that are related biologically even though there was no emotional connection (at least not originally). Do you think children who have the same biological father are truly "family"? Why or why not? Which do you think is most important—"nature" or "nurture"?

59

WHAT IS A FAMILY?

Find Out More

BOOKS

Burchell, Stephanie. *Whose Family Values?: A Study of Values and Family Life Among Traditional and Non-Traditional Parents.* Saarbrücken, Germany: VDM Verlag, 2008.

Coontz, Stephanie. *The Way We Never Were: American Families and the Nostalgia Trap.* Rev. New York: Basic Books, 2000.

Covey, Stephen R. *The 7 Habits of Highly Effective Families.* New York: Golden Books, 1997.

Gore, Al and Tipper. *Joined at the Heart: The Transformation of the American Family.* New York: Henry Holt, 2002.

Hansen, Karen V. *Not-So-Nuclear Families: Class, Gender, and Networks of Care.* Piscataway, N.J.: Rutgers University Press, 2005.

Lynette, Rachel. *What Makes Us a Family?: Living in a Nontraditional Family.* Edina, Minn.: Abdo Publishing, 2009.

Mason, Mary Ann, Arlene Skolnick, and Stephen D. Sugarman, eds. *All Our Families: New Policies for a New Century.* 2nd ed. New York: Oxford University Press, 2002.

Mitchell, Linda E. *Family Life in the Middle Ages.* Santa Barbara, Calif.: Greenwood, 2007.

Find Out More

Ojeda, Auriana. *The Family (Opposing Viewpoints).* Farmington Hills, Mich.: Greenhaven Press, 2003.

Pipher, Mary. *The Shelter of Each Other.* New York: Riverhead Books, 2008.

Volo, James M. and Dorothy Denneen Volo. *Family Life in Native America.* Santa Barbara, Calif.: Greenwood, 2007.

ON THE INTERNET

Berkeley Parents Network: All Kinds of Families
parents.berkeley.edu/advice/allkinds

Council on Contemporary Families
www.contemporaryfamilies.org

Family Diversity: Its How We Live
http://www.unmarriedamerica.org/family-diversity/entry.htm

Family Diversity Projects
www.familydiv.org

Harvard Family Research Project
www.hfrp.org

WHAT IS A FAMILY?

Bibliography

Carlson, Gail R. and M. Kathy Dothage. "Family Scene 13: Tips to Strengthen Families." University of Missouri Extension. October 1993. http://extension.missouri.edu/publications/DisplayPub.aspx?P=MP623. Accessed June 23, 2009.

"Communes Go to Court." *Time*. Feb. 1, 1971. http://www.time.com/time/magazine/article/0,9171,909763,00.html.

Schrader, Lucy. "What Makes a Family Strong?" MissouriFamilies.org: Parenting. May 5, 2009. http://missourifamilies.org/FEATURES/parentingarticles/parenting25.htm.

Toynbee, Polly. "What Makes a Happy Family?" *The Independent*. Jan. 17, 1994. http://www.independent.co.uk/opinion/what-makes-a-happy-family-polly-toynbee-explains-what-research-can-and-cannot-tell-us-about-the-children-of-lone-parents-1407474.html. Accessed June 22, 2009.

"What do you think makes a happy family?" CBBC Newsround. May 9, 2008. http://news.bbc.co.uk/cbbcnews/hi/newsid_6540000/newsid_6549400/6549495.stm.

"When Is a Family Not a Family?" *Toledo Blade*. Jan. 5, 1994. http://news.google.com/newspapers?nid=1350&dat=19940105&id=ZIAUAAAAIBAJ&sjid=WQMEAAAAIBAJ&pg=6234,1158372.

Index

abuse 29
adopt 12, 15, 23, 24, 31, 46
aunt 11, 114, 15, 45

baby 23, 49, 50, 59
   boom 12
      sitter 14

change 15, 27, 34, 42
cousin 11
church 22–25

daughter 49
divorce 9, 13, 19, 22, 37, 38, 40, 41, 51

extended 11, 47, 50

father 9, 14, 19, 20, 25, 40, 47, 49–51, 53, 54, 56, 58
foster 27

grandparent 11, 14–16, 25

heterosexual 23
homosexual 23

infant 25, 26

job 18, 38

kin 42, 45

love 12, 15, 30, 35, 46, 50

married 8–10, 12–15, 19, 20, 22, 23, 31, 38, 39, 50
monk 23, 24
mother 9, 15–18, 23, 38, 40, 48–52, 54, 58
multiracial 23

nuclear 10, 11, 46
nun 23, 24

pregnant 22, 23, 42

remarried 9, 20

same-sex 9, 23, 27, 31, 43
school 13–15, 40, 48, 51
son 15, 58
stepparent 16, 20
surname 14

uncle 11, 14, 45

WHAT IS A FAMILY?

About the Author and the Consultant

AUTHOR
Sheila Stewart has written several dozen educational books for young people. She lives with her children in Western New York and works as a writer and editor.

CONSULTANT
Gallup has studied human nature and behavior for more than seventy years. Gallup's reputation for delivering relevant, timely, and visionary research on what people around the world think and feel is the cornerstone of the organization. Gallup employs many of the world's leading scientists in management, economics, psychology, and sociology, and its consultants assist leaders in identifying and monitoring behavioral economic indicators worldwide. Gallup consultants help organizations boost organic growth by increasing customer engagement and maximizing employee productivity through measurement tools, coursework, and strategic advisory services. Gallup's 2,000 professionals deliver services at client organizations, through the Web, at Gallup University's campuses, and in forty offices around the world.